DREAMS ON

A COLLECTION OF MY WORKS. POETIC STORIES, POETRIES AND QUOTES.

HARSH MISHRA

Made with ♥ on the Notion Press Platform
www.notionpress.com

A Tribute to my dearest Dada Ji.

(I know you are looking at me from above and smiling.)

To Chotu Bhaiya & Vikas Sir,

To Mammi, Papa, Bhai.

And to Shriya (My Muse)!!!

Contents

Contents

Preface

We often feel this. Don.t we?

While watching a movie…

when a scene comes where a character's going through the same phase of life in which we find ourselves.

We connect with them hoping we can find some answers.

But guess what?

Eventually, their story ends somehow… But what about us?

What about our story?

"Jo Mai Agar Kitaabo'n Mein Jaa Ke Bas Jaau'n,
Na Hoke Yaha'n Bhi Mai'n Hazaaron Saal Jee Jaau'n!"
:- Harsh Mishra

DIVINE EYES

When the sun from the east arise,

Before ev'n a yawn, praise thine eyes.

To gleam! The moon takes your advice,

Then she says... Thine eyes, divine eyes!

Those eyes... Those divine eyes, such wise

Those lectors, made me realize...

Neither to hold grudge, nor disguise

Forgives all... Thine eyes, Divine Eyes!

They search for beauty in world,

But in them, art and beauty lies.

For what is there in the world

than except... ***THINE EYES, DIVINE EYES!***

SPONTAENITY

It's a scene of a party.

Back then I used to write little.

I was not aware of my writing capabilities.

Then at that party, I saw this girl.

She was gorgeous!

A friend of mine introduced me to her.

She asked me What did I do?

In a flow of framing my impression, I introduced myself as...

"I romanticise, sometimes immortalise, as I am a Poet!"

"Whoa!", she exclaimed surprisingly and asked, "Then tell me do I look like someone you can romanticise or immortalise?"

"Of course, you do!", I slipped it through that same flow of impressing her.

Though, at that very moment, I knew I can not write a great, not even good, poem right now.

So, I started scanning my mind for whatever beautiful stuff or beauty-related knowledge I had of different goddesses. Because it was on my 'Male-Ego', then!

"Then please, make me immortal.", she said and laughed but I saw it in her eyes that she wanted me to,

at least, say a few good lines about her, if not of great immortal quality.

So, I started with...

"Have you seen the eyes of Lakshmi?

So peaceful, serene and deep!

Well, yours stand close to them.",

'Not a hyperbole this big!' Echoed in my mind and I continued with...

"I wish to stay in them as those eyelashes make me feel Saraswati's acoustic!"

'Maintain the balance', Echoed again and I proceeded with...

"But worry not as I not only see Hindu Scriptures in you,

I see the beauty of the whole world in you.

Your awesome forehead depicts Irmina's courage.

Curves represent Aphrodite herself.

And why only women...

Even Cupid yearns for your shoulders as feathers

and here I thank Jove or Vishnu for even allowing me to witness this beauty...

While keeping Zeus unaware of thee!".

I ended.

She stood stunned,

"And what does all this mean? I understood only Lakshmi, Saraswati and Vishnu.", she asked.

"Umm, nothing, just romanticised you, I guess!"

I winked and laughed!

~

When thy face reflected its beauty on my eyes,

All the hyperbole written on love seemed true.

THY NECK

My fingers below that vector

Thy hypnotic neck, my nectar.

The sweet flute I wanna breathe through,

In Shiva's vein, where passes blue.

Behind those listening wings where

I want to kiss, if I may dare

And want to glide over that scent.

If a sin, I'd hourly repent.

Dawn of thy desired carving

I wish to read, make me lector.

To touch, feel, kiss, I am starving,

Thy hypnotic neck, my nectar.

SOUVENIR

We were wandering around a place I used to visit a lot when she was not in my life. I thought of taking her now with me because isn't she the person I love the most? Yes, she is! While sitting beneath a random tree she asked me a non-random question...

"What would you do if somehow I am no more here?", She asked.

"Why the hell are you saying this?", I argued.

"Because no one knows what the future holds and I can promise my life to you but there are some things that I can't promise which are not in my hand.", She answered. And her answer suggested DEATH which is not in anyone's hand, which can happen to anyone at any time!

I understood her point and responded with... "I know my answer to this, though that time will be so hard on me yet I know how to make you come to me, how to feel you! But you are a step luckier if the same happens to you!", I said.

"Wait, why? Why am I a step luckier if you won't be here?", she asked.

"Because there are things where I am still beheld!", I said.

"Where?", she asked.

"Did you forget I am a writer?", I queried.

"Yep, I seem to remember that!" She answered trying sarcasm.

"So yeah, there are a lot of pieces of me in my writings.", I said.

"Okay and...?" She signalled the question.

"And you just have to read those writings and you'll find me there! I am there and you remember my favourite tree, no, Which I've hugged many times... That tree kept my hug alive all this time and will be kept for infinity! And if you'll hug that tree, you'll hug me!" I answered.

"Yeah, you're right! And this answer of yours brought a new realisation to my mind.", She said.

"And what's that?", I asked.

"That is, if that tree and writings of yours can keep you alive in them from all this time to infinity then aren't we both the biggest impressions of ourselves, we both are our souvenirs! We'll keep ourselves alive in us from now to infinity!", she said.

"Yes, you are right my Souvenir! You will keep me alive in you and I will keep you alive in me!", I said feeling the happiest by her answer.

~

Memories replay the stories,

And the pain remains…

GOODNESS ME!

Goodness me, how it has now come to an end.

There!

I just began to love and... here!

My emotions are a dead letter.

Time... My dear cheaters! Will show me real faces.

Steps ahead of you

When you will be here

You will find my footprints

All here, set like a tier.

Had skin in the game,

I never disappear...

Careful, my teachers...

There's always a ready bier.

MODERN LOVE

"Gosh! Your smile... It even warms my cheeks up.", I said.

As we were having a video chat because she lives in a different town and our long-distance relationship had just started.

"Really? Thank you so much!", she replied.

"What? Just a thank you? And you're looking as if your mind is somewhere else. Tell me, what happened, is everything alright?", I asked in a curious tone.

"Nothing, it's just there's something I wanted to tell you for 2 days.", she replied.

"What? 2 days? What happened? Tell me?", I said and she started telling me about it.

"Someone's troubling me!", I interrupted asking about the person and she replied with...

"There's a boy who saw me in the college, I was looking at him and he got the wrong idea, I guess. And after that, he started coming after me, tried to meet me, he even caught my hand at a corner in the gallery and kissed my cheek, yesterday.", she said.

I replied in anger why didn't she do anything about that or slap him or complain or let me know? She was quiet and didn't respond to my question, so I calmed myself down and asked 'what happened then?' She replied with...

"Nothing till now...", she heard some noise then and ran towards her door while saying that she will call me later but the phone call was not off and I saw a man entering the house while having his hands around her waist, he was kissing her on the lips while she was having her hands only on his chest as if she was trying him to stop but he didn't even let her speak and as I saw that I started yelling at him and felt helpless but I saw her earphones were dropped on the floor by mistake.

Then, I saw him pushing her towards the right where the bed was being placed and I was shouting then I thought, I should call her again. But thought again that he won't let her pick and will switch it off.

Then, that man came to the left smiling and closed the main door and again jumped onto the bed.

It was then, that I listened to her voice giggling and she said...

"Come to me!", then her voice of giggling and panting started murdering me.

It was as if she is a cold-blooded murderer, slicing me slowly while enjoying it.

I don't even know why I stayed, I think I was dead then, couldn't even move my finger.

I was in trauma, or I don't know what.

But when the process of torturing me went off, she realised if I am alive or not.

So, she came in front of her camera and caught me smiling at her.

She said... "Sorry, sorry, sorry... I thought I ended the call."

~

IT'S LIGHTENING WHILE GETTING DAWN,

LIKE YOU, (MY MOON), WERE LOST TO SIGHT.

HOPELESS LOVE

A hope I bring with my heart,

That there is a mysterious girl.

Whose thoughts are ready to be freed,

Like a flight of butterflies.

Who wants to shine like a moon,

Even after the sun's rays burn.

Whose heart defines the love itself.

For her, I can wait for a thousand years.

Even after being acknowledged that,

This hope is hopeless!

ABEL

Country road.

Continental GT.

Fuel, Full.

Speed, 40.

Playlist, Shuffle.

Theher Ja from October Starts playing...

[He dreams.]

Abel. [Echoes.] Hey! Yeah, just over there. Thanks for the lift.

He. Your name?

Abel. Abel. [Pause.] Yours?

He. And... what's your real name?

Abel. [Chuckles.] Anvi! But you'll call me Abel.

He. Why?

Abel. You'll know.

[Both smile.]

Speed, 70.

Song, Tum Ho from Rockstar.

Abel. That was a nice proposal.

He. Only because you said yes.

[Both laugh and look at each other.]

Abel. Love you!

He. Love you, a lot! [Smiles.] So, when are you flying tomorrow?

Abel. 7:45 in the morning. Why?

He. Nothing. I'll be coming to drop you off because my office will be at 10 tomorrow.

Abel. Okay. And after I'll be back, we plan our wedding. Okay?

He. On your knees, madam.

Abel. Not knees. My head, your shoulder. Always! [Kisses his forehead.]

Speed, 90.

Song, Choo Lo from The Local Train.

A speedy bike passes by.

He. Slow, you stupid! Slow!!!

Abel. [Accelerating the bike to 90MPH.] No!!! Why fear? When you can hug me tight.

He. [Shouting.] It's neither your Airplane nor a runway.

Abel. Okay! [Slows down to 30MPH.] Why do you always fear speed? Feel it.

He. I don't know. I start losing my breath.

Abel. [Chuckels.] Haha! You reminded me of our honeymoon night when you lost your breath and I told you "I'm your breath, I'm your Abel!".

He. Yeah, it took you our wedding to tell me the meaning of your name... names!

Abel. You could have googled it.

He. You told me not to. You made me promise that when I asked you.

Abel. Yeah, father named me after the goddess of forest and...

He. [Interrupting.] ...you named yourself after air/breath. I know, I remember.

Speed, 120.

Song, Aaoge Tum Kabhi from The Local Train.

A bird passes.

He. A bird.

Abel. [From Computer Screen.] What?

He. A bird. A beautiful bird is outside our window.

Abel. Click and send.

He. Sent already. [Pause.] When will you be back? It's been more than a month, now.

Abel. Just three more days. A pilot got himself injured in the eye. So, they are sending me instead.

Speed, 150.

He. Why? Can't anyone else go?

Abel. Baby! It's only three days. Tomorrow I'll leave. Then the other day back. Then to you.

He. Don't go. Just come, no.

Abel. Don't worry. I'll be back and I also have a surprise for you. You're going to love it.

Speed, 180.

Song, Tab Bhi Tu from October.

A child comes in the way.

Everything seems slow.

Present.

He. You know I was afraid. Afraid of speed. Afraid of dying. Afraid of living. But by loving you, I have lived... With you, I learnt not to be afraid. But sometimes, I think that from me, you should have learnt, too. To be a little afraid. I am angry at you. You were a fighter, a fighter pilot. But who let you decide that our child, too? But now, this anger and fear. All have gone. Only love and shallow. Shallow. Empty. Missing.

Speed, 0.

Song, Meeting place from Rockstar.

Lying, Bleeding.

A little conscious.

An Airplane in the sky.

[Echoes.]

Doctor. Autopsy reports say she was pregnant.

Abel. Don't worry. I'll be back and I also have a surprise for you. You're going to love it.

Abel. I'm your breath, I'm your Abel.

[Present.]

He. I'm losing you, Abel. But, don't want to. I'm coming to you. To get my Abel. And her surprise. I want that surprise. See, you were a fighter, but I'm not. I can not fight this world, this shallowness, this loneliness. I need you. I'm coming to you, my Abel. My Anvi. My breath.

~

POETRY IS LIFE, LIFE IS CHAOS,

CHAOS IS SHE, AND I, A POET.

A BOOK

Oh! there was a girl...

A girl I always dreamt of…

She is like a book,

a book with an attractive cover.

Her eyebrows are like the strokes of those cursive letters on the title.

She's a book I imagine to read... and fancy to hold all the time.

Her actions are beautiful quotes, her thoughts, are the thoughtful words put in the places faultlessly that I crave to feel.

When she comes closer to me!

It feels like the rising action of the story by which, I get cold shivers but what relaxes me is the warmth of her presence.

And when she goes... huh!

It's the saddest ending which I won't be able to forget ever!

However, I lost her, as I tried to buy the book.

But, I found her glimpses, as I wrote to her.

Many beginnings and endings will come.

But the story of her arrival and our separation...

will remain in my heart, forever!

SHIMMERING LOVE

It's raining here and now these drops have made me remember a beautiful time.

I was driving alone and suddenly it rained. I stopped by a cafe to take shelter and they had this sitting area outside their cafe which was empty except for a girl. She was sitting there, first I didn't notice her as I was busy getting my phone and wallet settled up. And when I unplugged my earphones from my ears, I heard this famous old song playing in a low voice, which captured my attention quickly...

It was "Kabhi-Kabhi Kuch to Kaho Piya Hum se, Ay Kum Se Kum Aaj to Khul ke Milo Zara Hum se", from "Baahon Mein Chale Aao" by the great Lata Mangeshkar.

And then I turned my head towards the music and there she was playing this song on her phone while enjoying her coffee, it made me happy knowing there is a girl with good taste in music.

I ordered a coffee, too. And then the song switched to another beautiful one.

It was "Saiyyan" by Kailash Kher, which is a heart-melting piece that too during rains is something heavenly.

I was surprised by her choice of songs and quite impressed.

I ordered a Maggie, and then she again switched to the next song which was "Zaroori Tha" by Rahat Fateh Ali Khan.

Now, I don't know why but it felt like I, too, want to show how good my music taste is. So, I took off my phone and played "Aao Milon Chalein" by Shaan.

She noticed me and I don't know why but took it as a challenge and switched her song to "Sokhiyo Mein Ghola Jaaye" by Lata Mangeshkar.

Her eyes threw a glimpse of the competition and she was like 'I won'.

So, I changed my song to "Teri Deewani" by Kailash Kher.

And then we went on changing songs one by one as a competition.

She played "Tum Tak" by Javed Ali & A.R. Rehman.

I played "Saajna" by Falak Shabbir.

We were just playing a few lines from each song and started changing songs rapidly just after listening to each other's selection.

She played "Alag Aasmaan" by Anuv Jain.

I played "Waqt Ki Baatein" by Dream Note.

Then, It was like one on one round competition. She plays one good song and then if I play another one better than that, I win the round.

She played "Pasoori" by Ali Sethi.

I played "Jhoom" by Ali Zafar.

Then She played "Hosh Walon Ko Khabar Kya" by the great Jagjit Singh and in response to that, I stopped playing.

Because who am I to challenge the supremacy of that with any other songs now? Yeah, of course, it was a fun time competing with each other but then our eyes met during that song's line…

“Unse Nazrein Kya Mili, Roshan Fizaayein Ho Gayi”, (And then the humming part of the song teased us in the cutest way.), and by these lines… “Aaj Jaana Pyar Ki Ye, Jaadugari Kya Chiz Hai.”

We understood we have got something that we want to hold on to in our life just like that beautiful moment.

Wind blowing, Rains Falling, Birds Chirping, Trees Dancing, Jagjit Singh Singing, Eyes Meeting, Heart Melting, Love Happening, etc.

Then we enjoyed that whole song looking at everything and then she stood up, came towards me and sat beside me. And as she sat the song eventually got switched to "Tum Hi Ho" by the great Arijit Singh, and we both started laughing.

And now here I am aged around 56 remembering those beautiful times when my wife and I first met who is sitting beside me now and we are listening to the lines "Hum, Rahein Ya Na Rahe Kal, Pal... Yaad Aayenge Yeh Pal. Pal, ye hain Pyaar ke pal… chal, aa mere sang chal. Chal, soche hain kya? Choti si hai Zindagi. Kal, mil jaaye to hogi khushnasibi." from "Pal" by the great KK (Krishnakumar Kunnath).

~

LOVE FADED OUR COLOURS AND I BECAME A SILHOUETTE,

AGAINST THE DIMMING SKY OF YOUR FAKE PROMISES.

A DOOR

A DOOR LOCKED YET,

A DOOR I CAN'T LOCK

HAVEN'T FOUND A DOOR YET,

A DOOR I CAN'T LOCK.

A DOOR SOMETIMES AN END,

AN ENTERPRISE BEGINS BY SAME.

HAS THE POWER TO CHANGE MOODS,

CAN BRING SORROW, FALL, EVEN FAME.

SO MANY THINGS, A DOOR DOES...

YET VERY UNDERRATED.

A WALL BETWEEN TWO DIMENSIONS,

OR WORLD, ON IT WE ARE DEPENDED.

ALL MINE MEANS...

There is this girl... She's all mine!

All mine means... Umm!

All mine!!!

Her soul, her body, her actions, her hair...

Her legs, eyes, lips...

Her forehead and hands are only mine!!!

She went outside our hotel room to roam the gallery.

I went behind her to see what she was doing.

And she started walking towards another end of the lobby which has a window showing the street.

She went dancing like a kid interrupting anything she can interrupt.

Stretching the wires, beating the ground, patting the wall, wiping the railings...

She just went on with her chilled flow.

Then she finally reached the window and stood silent, straight and took a view of the world. Then she laughed at something which she saw through the window.

I knew at that very moment, that now she was going to return to me and will acknowledge me for what she saw. She turned back and started coming to me dancing, again!

Jumping on the ground, wiping the railings, patting the wall, stretching the ropes...

She reached to me and said...

"You know what I just saw?", She queried.

"Tell me!", I said.

"There's this cloth shop out there which has jeans on a dummy for ages and I saw that and wondered when are they going to sell that piece. Or the dummy has bought it?", She said and started laughing.

She made me laugh, too.

And that's when my heart exclaimed again!

Ugh! This girl...

This cute, little, elder, childish girl, Is all mine!

~

And when I feel you…

…I heel me!

LEFT

"You are with someone else now,

your friends told me.",

I said.

"And you believed them?",

She asked.

"No, I didn't!",

I said.

"And you won't, ever!"

She disclosed leaving me in my dream.

All alone!

Again!

A 3AM CONVERSATION

Hello! You there?

- (Ignoring) Hmm!

Hey! Wake up!

- (Ignoring) Hmm!

Wa-a-ke up, you!!!

-Who are you this late, again?

I'm your brain speaking.

-Why? (Frustrated) Will you ever stop speaking or thinking, please?

Why? What have I done?

- (Annoyed) Can't you just remain silent or shut yourself down?

Then how will you live?

-Ugh! Stop frustrating me! And tell me why do you want me to wake up while leaving this peaceful sleep?

Nothing, it's just that there is an emergency and I need your help.

-What? I never even had a girlfriend so no breakup and any emotional breakdown!!!

It's not tha-a-t! You and your girls... There are more important things!

-What are those? Will you tell me, now?

Yeah, sure! Just like this leg vein cramp you're just having inside your right leg.

-What-a-t? Ouch!!! (Realising and feeling hurt at the same time). Then send some hot blood there, you dammit.

Roger that! I've done it...

Now, will you please apply some oils and rub them,

you dammit!

~

A DRUGGIE GETS HIGH,

A POET… HIGHEST!

I

I ain't a dead letter!

I ain't a preach to deaf ears!

I ain't a dime a dozen!

I've removed my Achilles heel!

All who left me realized that they had backed the wrong horse!

But keep your regrets, I'm long gone, now!

For years, I haven't seen square one,

For my core hasn't changed.

Living life is like biting the bullet…

And I, Myself, Am the Gun!

SAY WHAT?

They were sitting on a couch in his room. His roommates left thinking if they needed some time alone.

They were feeling so good at that moment, both of them drowning in each other's eyes...

Their faces have this confidence to show that they are ready one more time for all that pain, jealousy, heartbreak or love!

They, still, are confused about what is there in the other person's mind while the girl asked...

'Which one of us is going to say that first?'

'Say what?" The boy replied playfully as he knew what is she exactly asking.

"You know exactly what I am asking!" The girl said. "You know this, too, that we are still friends and have started loving each other."

"Yes, I know that we are falling!", He said.

"No, not falling. I've fallen!", She said.

He denied it and told her to follow his gestures as he started to explain they have not fallen for each other yet.

He told her to look at his fingers and said, “See, this first finger is me and the second one is you... And we are falling and we are in this together.”

Listening to this, the girl dreadfully indicated towards his gestures that, soon, they are going to hit the ground if they are falling and it may again be a heartbreak.

To which the boy turned his fingers 180° and explained,

“Sorry! I forgot, to say, that whenever two people fall in love equally with each other, they fall upwards.

But when one of them leaves the other, then gravity replaces love.

And both hit the ground!”

~

People fell out of me...

And I became a rainbow!

Because we can!

Bro so much happened, no?

-Yet, we are here and breathing!

But, so many died!

-Many are living, too!

But, most of them lost!

-Many are fighting, Me too!

But, this year got us all stuck!

-It's not just this year, it's from when we were born.

But, I am losing now... And I am feeling low!

-Then why do you still have the strength to continue?

BE PATIENT

DECIDED ON THE TIME TO MEET.

IT'S RARE TO MEET IN THIS KIND OF LOVE, WHICH PEOPLE CALL LONG DISTANCE.

I CAME EARLY SO THAT SHE COULDN'T HAVE TO HOLD UP FOR ME.

BUT SHE CAME LATE FROM HER GIVEN TIME.

AND TO TEASE HER, I HID NEAR HER.

HER EYES WENT LOOKING FOR ME, BUT THEY HAD TO COME HOME

EMPTY-HANDED.

THEN SHE JUST DIALLED ME.

I SAW HER IMPATIENT EYES AND REACHED FOR HER RIGHT AWAY.

BUT I REMEMBER THAT SHE ASKED, "WHERE WAS I?".

INSTEAD OF FEELING MY PRESENCE.

AND ALL THIS MEMORY COMES TO ME,

MAKING ME FEEL THE MEANING OF PATIENCE IN RELATIONSHIPS.

IT CLARIFIES THAT,

THAT LOVE IS NOT LOVE

WHICH HAS TO BE LOVED.

AND ASKS ME A QUESTION,

COULDN'T HER LOVE WAIT FOR ME,

OR WAS I NOT EVEN LOVED?

~

AND WHEN YOU LEFT, MY HEART CRIED THE LOUDEST,

AS AN OWL'S FLAPPING WINGS.

WITH YOU!

DO YOU KNOW WHAT I LOVE THE MOST THESE DAYS?

WHEN I MISS YOU A LOT, INSTEAD OF BEING SAD,
WHILE LOOKING AT THE MOON,

I SEE OUR PICTURES ON THESE LONELY NIGHTS.

THEN I PLAY A TUNE, WHICH WE BOTH LOVED ONCE.

AND WHILE LISTENING TO THAT...

WHILE LOOKING AT THOSE PICTURES,

CARRYING A HEAVY HEART IN MILD PAIN, SLOWLY
CLOSING MY EYES,

I SMILE!

THEN THAT ONE DROP OF MY HEART'S UNHEARD
CRY FALLS ON MY FACE

FROM AN EYE OF MINE,

SEPARATING ME FROM THE FEELING OF YOU BEING
HERE.

SO A LONG BUT INTENSE BREATH I TAKE!

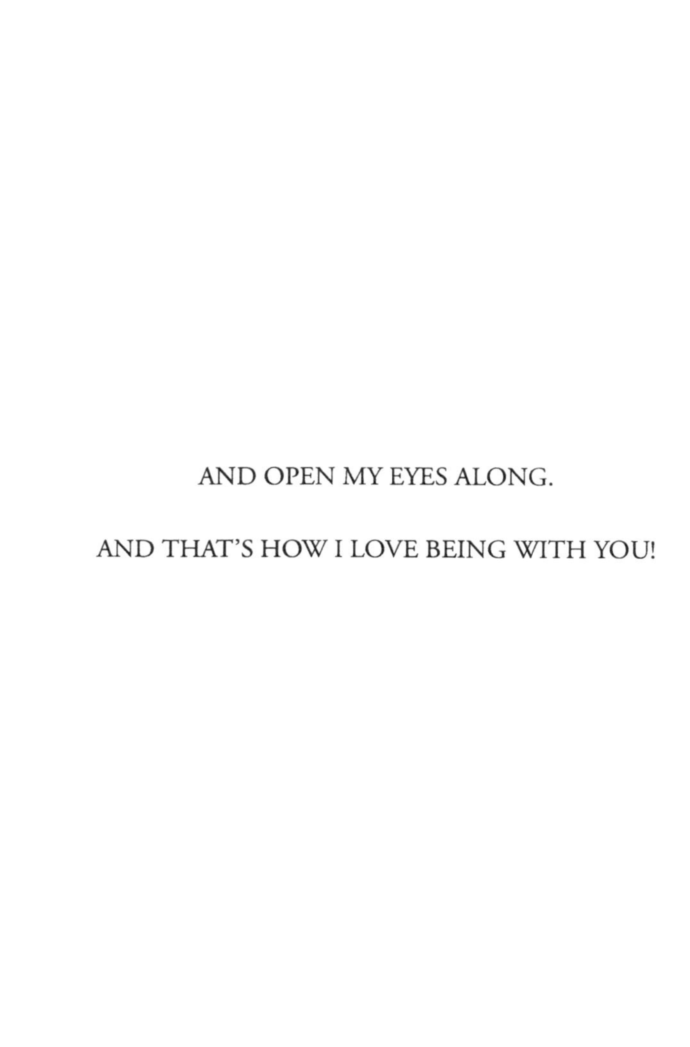

AND OPEN MY EYES ALONG.

AND THAT'S HOW I LOVE BEING WITH YOU!

VIZAG

(BASED ON A TRUE STORY)

WINTER.

We were on a trip to Visakhapatnam with a large number of friends.

We booked a bus to visit all the tourist sites. While discovering the whole of Vizag together we didn't know that we were about to witness a beautiful, magical and filmy evening, as well.

Our bus stopped near a tourist spot, it was a cave with lots of presentations inside. All of us jumped out and started walking toward the cave as it was far from the parking areas.

There were many shops for jewellery down the road and we wanted to check each of them. I bought her many things.

She was so happy. I, even, bought her our very first ring and put it on her finger. While doing all this window shopping, our friends reached the cave and we got left out.

But when we reached it, we saw the cost of entry per person, which seemed higher to us. We thought let's not go inside and just roam here and there a little. We started coming back towards our bus and for some time, sat while having us in each other's arms. It started getting dark.

Then started raining...

The coincidence was that eventually, I had my shrug with me which we both placed above our heads using it as an umbrella and ran for a safer place. We found a tea stall and went inside it. While the tea was in making, the time lost its pace for us and everything seemed slow. We looked at the reflection of our faces in each other's eyes which gleamed with the flames of love from inside. We kissed!

And as we kissed, the rain got slowed down. We've had our tea, so we thought we should go to the bus, now. While we approached the bus, we got a little wet. No one was there inside the bus except the driver in his seat. We went to our seats at the backside of the bus.

The driver turned on the colourful lights. We both felt... magical!

The windows of the bus were covered in fog and we wrote our names in them. I played music including our favourite "Alag Aasman" by Anuv Jain.

Then I noticed that she was wearing a bracelet which I just bought for her, went missing!

I asked her where is it. She said it might have fallen while running towards the bus and got sad about that because it was very beautiful.

I, too, was sad and decided that I must go and find that. Or else, buy a new one. She told me not to go out in that heavy rain and to sit with her, it's just a bracelet, we will buy a new one.

But I didn't listen to her and went outside.

Meanwhile, all of our friends returned and sat on the bus.

And when I returned with nothing, I saw one of our friends sitting next to her. Our relationship was private at that time. So, I was not able to say anything. He was only sitting there.

But I don't know why I got jealous and felt hurt. I was sitting alone in another seat. That taught me, I should have listened to her and stayed with her. And someone else is sitting in that place where I'm supposed to sit, now. Then, I woke up and went there and asked her that...

"Can I sit beside you?", she said yes. And the boy had to go away in a single seat. I gave priority to a lost bracelet over her request and left the bus. That taught me not to leave her, ever.

Or you will be left only with beautiful memories.

Which will do nothing but haunt.

~

You blew my darkness and despair...

Oh, you and I are a super pair!

9 798888 834589

Printed by Libri Plureos GmbH in Hamburg, Germany